D0367583

The Golfer's
Book of Wisdom

The Golfer's Book of Wisdom

Common Sense and Uncommon Genius From 101 Golfing Greats

Compiled and Edited by Criswell Freeman

WALNUT GROVE PRESS
Nashville, TN
(615) 256-8584

ISBN 0-9640955-6-4

The ideas expressed in this book are not, in all cases, exact quotations, as some have been edited for clarity and brevity. In all cases, the author has attempted to maintain the speaker's original intent. In some cases, material for this book was obtained from secondary sources, primarily print media. While every effort was made to ensure the accuracy of these sources, the accuracy cannot be guaranteed. For additions, deletions, corrections or clarifications in future editions of this text, please write WALNUT GROVE PRESS.

Printed in the United States of America
by Vaughan Printing, Inc.
Book Design by Armour&Armour
Cover Design by Bart Dawson
Typesetting & Page Layout by Sue Gerdes
Edited by Alan Ross
7 8 9 10 • 00 01 02 03 04 05

ACKNOWLEDGMENTS
The author gratefully acknowledges the helpful support of Mary Susan Freeman, Don Pippen, and all the writers who have chronicled the exploits and wisdom of golf's greatest players.

For Malcolm Firth and Randall Phillips

Great Golfers, Even Greater Friends

Table of Contents

Introduction

Countless words have been written about the game of golf. The shelves are filled with books by the likes of Nicklaus, Jones, Palmer, Hogan and Snead. Great players and teaching professionals have written books on putting, driving, swinging, and chipping. They've written about the long game, the short game, and the mental game. Why then another book about golf? In this text, I hope to share the wisdom of the sport. And what wonderful wisdom it is.

Golf combines mental discipline with physical skill in a unique way. On the links, physical ability means little if it is not accompanied by nerves of steel, clearheaded judgment, and years of practice. The best players may train for a quarter of a century before finally winning consistently at the highest levels.

Given the demanding nature of the sport, it is not surprising that the game's greatest players are, in their own ways, philosophers. The stoical approach of Nicklaus is reminiscent of the ancient sage Epictetus. Palmer's aggressive style reminds one of a great military leader (consider Arnie's Army). And Walter Hagen's pursuit of the good life models Epicurean philosophy.

The wisdom of golf's greatest players is not reserved for the first tee or the practice range. While the advice herein may indeed lower your handicap, don't relegate this book to your golf bag. Whether you're a scratch golfer or a rank beginner, you can profit from the common sense that follows. It is a philosophy not just of golf, but of life.

1

The Game of Golf

Why do we love the game of golf? It is a sport that combines the best that nature and man have to offer. Golf offers opportunities for relaxation, companionship, and accomplishment. Its rules are almost always self-enforced, making it a game of character and sportsmanship. The challenge of competition is present on every shot because the golfer competes not only with others, but also with himself. Who can deny the joy of a well-hit drive or the satisfaction of sinking a testy putt?

Golf also meets our need for heroes. One generation reveres Jones and Hagen, the next Palmer and Nicklaus. The mantle is passed to Watson, Norman, Ballesteros and then to Woods, while rising stars wait impatiently in the wings.

Champions reign all too briefly, but the greatness of golf endures.

Golf is the Great Mystery.

P. G. Wodehouse

Golf is a compromise between what your
ego wants you to do, what experience tells
you to do, and what your nerves
will let you do.

Bruce Crampton

No other game combines the wonder
of nature with the discipline of sport in such
carefully planned ways. A great golf course
both frees and challenges a golfer's mind.

Tom Watson

Golf is good for the soul. You get so mad at
yourself you forget to hate your enemies.

Will Rogers

If you watch a game, it's fun.
>   If you play it, it's recreation.
>   If you work at it, it's golf.

>> *Bob Hope*

Golf is the most human game of all.
>   You have the same highs and lows —
>   sometimes in the same round.

>> *Lee Trevino*

Golf is a day spent in a round
>   of strenuous idleness.

>> *William Wordsworth*

Golf has probably kept more people sane
>   than psychiatrists have.

>> *Harvey Penick*

Golf is deceptively simple
yet endlessly complicated.

Arnold Palmer

Golf is a game in which one endeavors
to control a ball with implements
ill adapted for the purpose.

Woodrow Wilson

Golf is a game of finding what works,
losing it, and finding it again.

Ken Venturi

Golf is the "only-est" sport.
You're completely alone with every
conceivable opportunity to defeat yourself.

Hale Irwin

Golf is a game
of endless predicaments.

Chi Chi Rodriguez

Professional golf is the only sport where,
if you win 20% of the time, you're the best.

Jack Nicklaus

Golf appeals to the idiot in us and the child.

John Updike

Golf is America's sport.

Lee Trevino

Golf is an ideal diversion but a ruinous disease.

B. C. Forbes

Golf is like a love affair.
If you don't take it
seriously, it's no fun;
if you do take it seriously,
it breaks your heart.

Arnold Daly

2

The Joy of Golf

Although the origins of golf are obscure, it seems clear that Scottish citizens were enjoying the game by the middle of the 15th century. Many things have changed since the day in 1457 when Parliament criticized the Scots for playing too much "golfe," but the game's amazing popularity has endured.

If you've been playing a little too much "golfe" lately, don't despair — you're not alone. The love of the links is 500 years old and still growing.

The Joy of Golf

Maintain a childhood enthusiasm
for the game of golf.

Chi Chi Rodriguez

There's a little kid in all of us.
The trick is knowing how to let
that child come out.

Mac O'Grady

It's not your life, it's not your wife,
it's only a game.

Lloyd Mangrum

The game is meant to be fun.

Jack Nicklaus

What other people may find
in poetry or art museums,
I find in the flight of a good drive.

Arnold Palmer

I'm a golfaholic.
>> And all the counseling in the world
>> wouldn't help me.

Lee Trevino

Euphoria is a perfectly executed heroic shot.

Robert Trent Jones, Jr.

Relax.
>> Enjoy the walk between shots.
>> That's your chance to loosen up
>> so your next shot is comfortable.

Julius Boros

You're never too old to play golf.
>> If you can walk, you can play.

Louise Suggs

In golf, while there is life, there is hope.

Sir Walter Simpson

The ardent golfer would play Mount Everest
if somebody would put a flagstick on top.

Pete Dye

Golf is like eating peanuts.
You can play too much or play too little.

Bobby Jones

I play the game. I enjoy it.
I don't let it devour me.

Gene Littler

Go play golf.
Go to the golf course.
Hit the ball.
Find the ball.
Repeat until the ball is in the hole.
Have fun.
The end.

Chuck Hogan

Don't play too much golf.
Two rounds
a day are plenty.

Harry Vardon

Hit the ball and when you find it,
    hit it again.

Don January

Keep your sense of humor.
There's enough stress in the rest of your life
    to let bad shots ruin a game
        you're supposed to enjoy.

Amy Alcott

You can think best when you're happiest.

Peter Thomson

Fun is your own creation.
        Create your own fun.

Chuck Hogan

Always keep it fun. If you don't have fun,
    you'll never grow as a person or a player.

Tiger Woods

The constant undying hope for
improvement makes golf
so exquisitely worth playing.

Bernard Darwin

Nobody plays golf for his health.
Of all the lame excuses people give
for playing the game, this one
is the most maladroit.

Charles Price

Golf is a great and glorious game.
Even those of us who earn our livings at it
play it more for the pleasure
than for the money.

Arnold Palmer

It's difficult to excel at something
you don't truly enjoy.

Jack Nicklaus

Practice, which some regard as a chore,
should be approached as just about the
most pleasant recreation ever devised.

Babe Didrikson Zaharias

Give it your best, but always with the
realization that your happiness and your
livelihood are not riding on the next shot.

Jane Blalock

The "click" of a solid wood shot soaring
far down the fairway is well worth all the
hours of practice.

Jimmy Demaret

Go out and have fun. Golf is a game for
everyone, not just for the talented few.

Harvey Penick

Enjoy the game.
Happy golf is good golf.

Gary Player

Don't take your bad shots home with you.

Tony Lema

3

Sound Advice

On the golf course, advice is everywhere. Go to any practice tee and ask the first person you see for help. You'll find no shortage of tips: Keep your head down, keep your elbow in, keep you arm straight, stay loose, concentrate, bend your knees, keep your balance, have a firm grip, don't hold the club too tightly, follow through, swing hard, swing easy, and so forth.

What follows is wise counsel from great players. It applies both on and off the course.

Always keep learning.
It keeps you young.

Patty Berg

Give luck a chance to happen.

Tom Kite

Know your strengths
   and take advantage of them.

Greg Norman

Never bet with anyone who has a deep tan,
   squinty eyes, and a one-iron in his bag.

Dave Marr

The most successful way to play golf
is the easiest way.

Harry Vardon

To play your best golf, be yourself.

Father's Advice to Tiger Woods

My strategy? Playing safe and within myself.

Billy Casper

If you play poorly one day, forget it.
If you play poorly the next time out,
review your fundamentals.
If you play poorly for a third time in a row,
see your professional.

Harvey Penick

Instead of worrying about making a fool
of yourself in front of a crowd of 4 or 40,000,
forget about how you look and concentrate
instead on where you want the ball to go.
Pretty is as pretty does.

Harvey Penick

Nobody asked how you looked,
just what you shot.

Sam Snead

If I had it to do over again,
I wouldn't beat myself up so much.

Gardner Dickinson

If you drink, don't drive. Don't even putt.

Dean Martin

Get a system of some kind in playing golf.
Any kind of system beats trusting luck.

Jack Burke, Sr.

Don't give advice unless you're asked.

Amy Alcott

I always advise people never to give advice.

P. G. Wodehouse

I don't recommend playing golf every day.
There is nothing worse in the world
than getting stale at one thing.

Gene Sarazen

I cling to a few tattered old virtues, like
believing you don't get anything in this world
for nothing. This is one of those eternal
verities that will be around long after
I've sunk my last putt and gone to
that great 19th hole in the sky.

Tony Lema

Only fools live in the past
    or carry envy into the present.

Chi Chi Rodriguez

Visualize winning.

Gary Player

Play golf to the hilt.
    Win, lose, or draw, good day or bad,
        you'll be happier for it,
        and you'll live longer.

Arnold Palmer

Always use a clean ball.

Harry Vardon

In choosing a partner,
always pick the optimist.

Tony Lema

Keep hitting it straight
until the wee ball
goes in the hole.

James Braid

4

Attitudes

In the game of golf, attitude is everything. Nowhere in the world of sport is the self-fulfilling prophesy more prevalent. The golfer who stands over a shot with hesitation and fear is doomed before he begins his backswing. The confident golfer, on the other hand, is more likely to execute a smooth, steady swing.

Bruce Crampton noted, "A good shot can do wonders for your attitude." It is worth adding that a good attitude can do wonders for your shot.

The proper golfing mind-set is a mixture of realism, optimism, determination, and composure. Consider the words of the following champions; then adjust *your* attitude accordingly.

Never tell yourself you can't make a shot.
Remember, we are what we think we are.

Gary Player

The first thing anybody has to do to be any
good at anything is believe in himself.

Gay Brewer

A buoyant, positive approach to the game
is as basic as a sound swing.

Tony Lema

Be decisive.
A wrong decision is generally less
disastrous than indecision.

Bernhard Langer

Golf is a matter of confidence.
If you think you cannot do it,
there is no chance you will.

Henry Cotton

Try to think where you want to put the ball
not where you don't want it to go.

Billy Casper

Sometimes the biggest problem is in your
head. You've got to believe you can play a
shot instead of wondering where your
next bad shot is coming from.

Jack Nicklaus

Golfers are the greatest worriers
in the world of sport.

Billy Casper

Worry is poison.

Peter Thomson

Don't load yourself up with additional
worries about the man setting the pace,
because he probably has troubles of his own.

Bobby Jones

To play well you must feel tranquil and at
peace. I have never been troubled by nerves
in golf because I felt I had nothing to lose
and everything to gain.

Harry Vardon

Some people think they are concentrating when they're merely worrying.

Bobby Jones

Most golfers prepare
for disaster.
A good golfer
prepares for success.

Bob Toski

You need a fantastic memory to remember
the great shots and a very short memory
to forget the bad ones.

Mac O'Grady

You play golf every week. You can take the
pressure off by reminding yourself there's
always next week. You can't do that in the
World Series or the Olympics.

Calvin Peete

You tend to get impatient with
less-than-perfect shots, but you have to
remember less-than-perfect shots win Opens.

Curtis Strange

The first step in building a solid, dependable attitude is to be realistic, not only about your inherent capabilities, but also about how well you are playing to those capabilities on any given day.

Byron Nelson

Confidence, without ability, is impossible to maintain. You can't feel confident very long if you don't know how to hit the ball.

Doug Ford

I don't blame the golf gods for a bad swing. I blame Chi Chi Rodriguez.

Chi Chi Rodriguez

Focus on remedies,
not faults.

Jack Nicklaus

Pop didn't just teach me golf.
He taught me discipline.

Arnold Palmer

The greatest single lesson to be learned
from golf is mental discipline.

Louise Suggs

What does it take to be a champion?
Desire, dedication, determination,
concentration, and the will to win.

Patty Berg

Winning golf is total commitment,
physically and mentally. If you feel you
are weak, you should be in the gym
developing your body for golf.

Nick Faldo

To win, you must treat a pressure situation
as an opportunity to succeed,
not an opportunity to fail.

Gardner Dickinson

Don't look for excuses to loose.
Look for excuses to win.

Chi Chi Rodriguez

A bad attitude is worse than a bad swing.

Payne Stewart

I don't dwell on bad shots, bad rounds,
or bad tournaments. I don't play in the past.
I play in the present.

Raymond Floyd

Do your best,
one shot at a time
and then move on.
Remember that
golf is just a game.

Nancy Lopez

5

Adversity

The British wordsmith P. G. Wodehouse once observed that, "Golf acts as a corrective measure against sinful pride." Even the game's greatest players can be humbled as they attempt to send that small white ball toward its target. The seasoned golfer knows that trouble waits patiently for the untrained, the unwise, or the unlucky.

No round of golf is without adversity — it is a game of hazards, traps, and penalties. Consequently, golfers have much to say about hardship. Take the following words of wisdom to heart. They apply whether trouble occurs in the game of golf *or* the game of life.

Adversity is the fork in the road.
 You'll get better or you'll get worse,
 but you'll never stay the same.

Ken Venturi

Only in America can I sign a wrong card
 and become a national hero.

Roberto De Vicenzo

Start each hole with an awareness that
there may be subtle or mysterious elements
 waiting to sabotage your game.

Robert Trent Jones, Jr.

To be consistently effective, you must put a
 certain distance between yourself and
 what happens to you on the golf course.
 This is not indifference—it's detachment.

Sam Snead

One bad shot does not make a losing score.

Gay Brewer

Every golfer can expect to have
four bad shots a round. When you do,
just put them out of your mind.

Walter Hagen

As I get older, I try to think of the
bad things that happen to me on the golf
course as "tests." They're not hurdles;
they're not bad marks or punishments.
They're things I need in my life,
things that bring me back to reality.

Frank Beard

Recovering from a bad hole can be the
difference between success and failure.

Gay Brewer

When you're playing poorly,
you start thinking too much.
That's when you confuse yourself.

Greg Norman

Thinking instead of acting is the
number one disease in golf.

Sam Snead

My reaction to anything that happens on
the golf course is no reaction.
There are no birdies or bogeys,
no eagles or double bogeys;
there are only numbers.
If you can learn that, you can play this game.

Jim Colbert

You can talk strategy all you want,
but what really matters is resiliency.

Hale Irwin

Focus not on the commotion around you, but on the opportunity ahead of you.

Arnold Palmer

Take your lies as they come.
Take the bad bounces with the good ones.

Ben Crenshaw

You are meant to play the ball as it lies,
a fact that may help to touch on
your own objective approach to life.

Grantland Rice

Good golfers learn to convert anger
into productivity.

Tommy Bolt

Champions control the violence
within themselves.

Bob Toski

The worse you're performing, the harder
you must work mentally and emotionally.
The greatest and toughest art in golf is
"playing badly well." All the true greats
have been masters at it.

Jack Nicklaus

Make the total effort,
even when the odds are against you.

Arnold Palmer

A hungry dog hunts best.

Lee Trevino

When in trouble,
play the shot you know you can play,
not the shot you hope you can play.

Jack Burke, Jr.

A bogey can be like a wake-up call.
It can snap you back mentally.

Peter Jacobsen

I like the feeling of trying my hardest
under pressure.

Tiger Woods

Every great player has learned the two Cs:
how to *concentrate* and
how to maintain *composure*.

Byron Nelson

No matter what happens,
keep on hitting the ball.

Harry Vardon

6

Sportsmanship & Character

The British historian Lord Macaulay noted that, "The measure of a man's real character is what he would do if he knew he would never be found out."

To fully appreciate the game of golf, one must meet Macaulay's test of integrity. Golf is a game that is built upon sportsmanship and honesty. Consider the following observations from true champions who have won with honor.

Golf is a game of integrity.

Raymond Floyd

True golfers police themselves.

Bruce Crampton

Golf is like solitaire. When you cheat,
you only cheat yourself.

Tony Lema

You might as well praise a man
for not robbing a bank as to praise
him for playing by the rules.

Bobby Jones

Golf puts a man's character on the anvil
and his richest qualities — patience, poise,
and restraint — to the flame.

Billy Casper

Golf is a game of honor.
If you're playing it any other way,
you're not getting the
fullest satisfaction from it.

Harvey Penick

Eighteen holes of golf will teach you more
about your foe than eighteen years
of dealing with him across a desk.

Grantland Rice

To find a man's true character,
play golf with him.

P. G. Wodehouse

I't's good sportsmanship to not pick up
   lost golf balls while they are still rolling.
Mark Twain

D'on't praise your own good shots.
Leave that function to your partner who, if a
good sport, will not be slow in performing it.
Harry Vardon

S'udden success in golf is like the sudden
   acquisition of wealth. It is apt to unsettle
   and deteriorate the character.
P. G. Wodehouse

Never needle, harass, or poke fun at a playing partner who's on the edge of despair.

Doug Sanders

Win graciously.

Arnold Palmer

Be brave if you lose and meek if you win.

Harvey Penick

Successful competitors want to win.
Head cases want to win at all costs.

Nancy Lopez

I never rooted against an opponent,
    but I never rooted for him either.

Arnold Palmer

I never pray that I may win.
    I just ask for the courage to do my best.

Gary Player

Success in golf depends
less on strength of body
than upon strength of
mind and character.

Arnold Palmer

7

Practice & Preparation

Ben Hogan wrote, "There are no born golfers. Some have more natural ability than others, but they've all been made." Hogan, known for his devotion to the practice tee, combined innate ability with relentless preparation. For his efforts, he was rewarded with championship after championship.

Whether it's school, the workplace, or the golf course, preparation is essential. Natural ability is a wonderful thing, but it doesn't guarantee success. In life, as in golf, there's no substitute for hard work.

You must work
very hard to become a
natural golfer.

Gary Player

Golf is assuredly a mystifying game.
It would seem that if a person has hit a golf
ball correctly a thousand times, he should be
able to duplicate the performance at will.
But this is certainly not the case.

Bobby Jones

You build a golf game like you build a wall,
one brick at a time.

Tony Lema

Don't be too anxious to see good results on
the scoreboard until you've fully absorbed
the principles of the golf swing
on the practice tee.

Louise Suggs

A couple of hours of practice
is worth ten sloppy rounds.

Babe Didrikson Zaharias

Preparation through steady practice is the
only honest avenue to achieving
your potential.

Chi Chi Rodriguez

Work on the fundamentals constantly.

Nick Price

The harder you work, the luckier you get.

Gary Player

There is nothing in this game of golf that
can't be improved upon — if you practice.

Patty Berg

The only way to build *realistic* confidence in
yourself is through practice.

Sam Snead

Every day you miss playing or practicing is one day longer it takes to be good.

Ben Hogan

They say "practice makes perfect."
Of course, it doesn't. For the vast majority of
golfers it merely consolidates imperfection.

Henry Longhurst

The most common practice error is to drift
aimlessly to the range and start banging balls
at random. This isn't practice. This is a waste
of time. The worst thing you can do
is practice your mistakes.

Tony Lema

Every time you go out to hit a bag of balls,
it should be for a definite purpose.

Dow Finsterwald

Never practice without a thought in mind.

Nancy Lopez

Every golfer has a fault he falls back into
repeatedly. The trick is learning what
that fault is and how to correct it.

Ken Venturi

Correct one fault at a time. Concentrate on
the one fault you want to overcome.

Sam Snead

When practicing, use the club that gives
you the most trouble, not the one
that gives you the most satisfaction.

Harry Vardon

Practice puts your brains in your muscles.

Sam Snead

My philosophy?
Practice, practice, practice — and win.

Babe Didrikson Zaharias

If you're serious about improving your play, be brutally honest with yourself.

Greg Norman

Anyone can learn the basics. A professional can teach you everything he knows in two hours. If you keep coming back, you're just rehearsing. Golf is a game of repetition, of practice, practice, practice.

Lee Trevino

It was a great joy to improve. There wasn't enough daylight in the day for me. I always wished the days were longer so I could practice and work.

Ben Hogan

What you might learn in six months of practice, your pro can tell you in five minutes.

Jack Burke, Sr.

Don't be too proud to take lessons. I'm not.

Jack Nicklaus

Make a game out of practice. You're still a child at heart.

Harvey Penick

8

The Mental Game

When Ralph Waldo Emerson noted that, "Life is a festival only for the wise," he could have been describing life on the links. The prudent golfer thinks ahead and avoids foolish risks. This sort of thoughtful play is good for one's spirit as well as one's handicap.

If you want to lower your score while increasing your enjoyment of the game, please take time to consider the following advice. These words of wisdom, if taken to heart, have the power to transform your golf game and your life.

You win major
tournaments with
your mind.

Tiger Woods

Golf is more in your mind than in your clubs.

Bruce Crampton

Once you have gained an effective,
repeatable swing, golf is played
almost entirely between the ears.

Seve Ballesteros

The mind messes up more shots
than the body.

Tommy Bolt

The difference between winning and losing
is always a mental one.

Peter Thomson

We create success or failure on the course
primarily by our thoughts.

Gary Player

Hitting the ball isn't all there is to golf.
The right mental approach can be just as
important as a golfer's swing.

Gay Brewer

The most important component of good golf
is the ability to concentrate.

Dow Finsterwald

Confidence in golf means being able to
concentrate on the problem at hand
with no outside interference.

Tom Watson

You can always find a distraction
if you're looking for one.

Tom Kite

Driving is about seventy-five percent mental,
so I believe in giving the ball some sweet talk
on the tee. "This isn't going to hurt a bit,"
I whisper under my breath. "Sambo is just
going to give you a little ride."

Sam Snead

The hardest thing in golf is controlling your
emotions. You're facing a dead-still object,
something you can only address with your
club after a long wait. Your hands are tied in
knots, your mind begins to wander.
You must find a release from the tension.

JoAnne Carner

Of all the hazards, fear is the worst.

Sam Snead

U.S. Opens are won with guts and pars.

Curtis Strange

Nervous tension is the biggest enemy in golf.

Sandra Haynie

Imagination is the death of a low golf score
if you visualize hazards that don't exist.

Gene Sarazen

Fear comes in two packages — fear of failure,
and sometimes, fear of success.

Tom Kite

The guys who do well are the ones
with the strongest mental outlook.

Justin Leonard

Use your brain, not your endurance.

Peter Thomson

Concentration is a fine antidote to anxiety.

Jack Nicklaus

If you have to remind yourself to concentrate
during competition, you have
no chance to concentrate.

Bobby Nichols

Discipline and concentration
>are a matter of being interested.

Tom Kite

Par golf is careful golf.

Doug Ford

Remember — you have to be comfortable.
Golf is *not* a life or death situation.
It's just a game and should be
treated as such. Stay loose.

Chi Chi Rodriguez

In golf you have to concentrate. My father
and my friends call it zoning. If you mishit
a shot, you have to get your focus back.
You have got to start thinking ahead.
Don't look behind.

Tiger Woods

Sometimes, thinking too much
can destroy your momentum.

Tom Watson

Through preparation and hard work,
you can prepare yourself for a
mental attitude — a "zone."
When it happens, all you see is
the ball and the hole.

Payne Stewart

Golf is a spiritual game. It's like Zen.
You have to let your mind take over.

Amy Alcott

Attain serenity in chaos. You cannot let
yourself be sabotaged by adrenaline.

Mac O'Grady

Think ahead. Golf is a next-shot game.

Billy Casper

It's one thing to be outplayed at golf,
and another to be outsmarted.

Doug Sanders

The guy who believes in happy endings is
going to play consistently better golf
than the man who approaches every act
of existence with fear and foreboding.

Tony Lema

9

The Swing

Until one has attempted it, the golf swing seems a simple task. The ball doesn't move. One has a wide choice of clubs and a lifetime to practice. But the golf swing is not so simple as it appears — many things can and do go awry.

Author John Updike observed, "The golf swing is like a suitcase into which we are trying to pack one too many items." The weekend hacker may fall prey to a wide variety of twists, twitches, and turns. With each extra motion comes an increased probability of errant shots.

Would you like to improve your score? Try packing a few less moves into your swing — and read on.

The Swing

Each player ought to have a style which is
the reflection of himself, his build, his mind,
his age, and his previous habits.

Sir Walter Simpson

The real road to improvement lies in gaining
a working knowledge of the correct swing
in general, and yours in particular.

Bobby Jones

There are no absolutes in golf.
Golf is such an individual game,
and no two people swing alike.

Kathy Whitworth

The ultimate judge of your swing is
the flight of the ball.

Ben Hogan

The accepted view is that the game of golf is complex, difficult, and inherently frustrating. I just don't buy that.

Arnold Palmer

Learn the fundamentals of the game and stick to them. Band-Aid remedies never last.

Jack Nicklaus

With a good grip, a little ability and a lot of desire, *anybody* can become good golfer.

Deacon Palmer

It's not just enough to swing at the ball. You've got to loosen your girdle and really let the ball have it.

Babe Didrikson Zaharias

Don't analyze your own swing.
The chances are you can't do it properly.
Have a pro do the job.

Sam Snead

Working on swing fundamentals is the
surest way to improve your game.

Nick Price

Reverse every natural instinct and do the
opposite of what you are inclined to do,
and you will probably come very close
to having a perfect golf swing.

Ben Hogan

Imagine the ball has little legs,
and chop them off.

Henry Cotton

You must swing smoothly to play golf well.
And you must be relaxed to swing smoothly.

Bobby Jones

No good player ever swings as hard as he can.
Power is a matter of timing,
not overpowering the ball.

Arnold Palmer

Don't press. You can hit hard without pressing.

Harry Vardon

Many shots are spoiled at the last instant
by efforts to add a few more yards.

Bobby Jones

The essence of good form is simplicity.

Bobby Jones

The simpler I keep things, the better I play.

Nancy Lopez

Make the basic shot-making decision early,
clearly and firmly, and then ritualize
all the necessary acts of preparation.

Sam Snead

If there is a doubt in your mind over
a golf shot, how can your muscles
know what they are expected to do?

Harvey Penick

You can't hit a good five-iron if you're
thinking about a six-iron on your back swing.

Charles Coody

Never have a club in your bag
that you're afraid to hit.

Tom Kite

Fight tautness whenever it occurs;
    strive for relaxed muscles throughout.

Bobby Jones

I believe most sincerely that the impulse
    to steer, born of anxiety, is accountable
      for almost every really bad shot.

Bobby Jones

Looking up is the biggest alibi ever invented
    to explain a terrible shot. By the time you
    look up, you've already made the mistake.

Harvey Penick

That was the worst
swing I ever heard.
Charley Boswell
Championship Blind Golfer

The Swing

A long drive is good for the ego.

Arnold Palmer

The best-stroked putt in a lifetime
   does not bring the aesthetic satisfaction
   of a perfectly hit wood or iron shot.

Al Barkow

When I think about three things
   during my swing I'm playing poorly;
   when I think about two things,
   I have a chance to shoot par;
   when I think of only one thing
   I could win the tournament.

Bobby Jones

I've seen enough crazy shots to know
   they happen in the best of families.

Lee Trevino

<u>10</u>

Course Management

American humorist Kin Hubbard once observed, "Lot's of folks confuse bad management with destiny." Often, we are tempted to blame the golfing gremlins for missed shots and high scores, but the truth usually hits closer to home. In the words of Shakespeare, "The fault, dear Brutus, lies not in our stars, but in ourselves."

The quickest way to lower your score is to manage your game. For some powerful pointers, turn the page. You'll improve your management style *and* your golfing destiny.

Success depends almost entirely on how
effectively you learn to manage
the game's two ultimate adversaries:
the course and yourself.

Jack Nicklaus

No two courses or rounds are ever so alike
that you can attack them with
exactly the same game plan.

Robert Trent Jones, Jr.

Golf is a thinking man's game.
You can have all the shots in the bag,
but if you don't know what to do with them,
you've got troubles.

Chi Chi Rodriguez

The ability to score well is not due
to perfection in swing. It takes a
combination of swinging and planning.

Doug Ford

Management — placing the ball in the right position for the next shot — is eighty percent of winning golf.

Ben Hogan

The key is playing the ball to the best position from which to play the next shot.

Arnold Palmer

Play every shot so that the next one will be the easiest that you can give yourself.

Billy Casper

You don't have the game you played last year or last week. You only have today's game. It may be far from your best, but that's all you've got. Harden your heart and make the best of it.

Walter Hagen

Smart golf is winning golf.
Cut down on the element of chance.

Walter Hagen

Reckless gambles add needless strokes.

Bob Goalby

In every case, there is a risk-reward factor.
The course forces you to evaluate each shot
in terms of nerve and skill. The more decisive
your shot selection and thought process, the
greater your chances of mastering the course.

Robert Trent Jones, Jr.

It doesn't matter how long you hit it.
You've got to be accurate.

Tiger Woods

In golf, there is no short cut to better scoring.
Better golf is attained through
infinite attention to detail.

Doug Ford

The toughest opponent of all is Old Man Par.
He's a patient soul who never shoots a birdie
and never incurs a bogey. He's a patient soul,
Old Man Par. And if you would travel the long
road with him, you must be patient, too.

Bobby Jones

Forget your opponents;
always play against par.

Sam Snead

More matches are lost through carelessness
at the beginning than any other cause.

Harry Vardon

The secret of low scores is the ability
to turn three shots into two.

Bobby Jones

Every shot counts. The three-foot putt
is just as important as the 300-yard drive.

Henry Cotton

It's just as important to sink a bogey putt
as it is to drop one for a par.

Doug Ford

Ask yourself how many shots you would
have saved if you never lost your temper,
never got down on yourself, always developed
a strategy before you hit, and always played
within your own capabilities.

Jack Nicklaus

If you can't hit a driver, don't.

Greg Norman

The short game.
Those are the magic words.

Harvey Penick

Heartaches usually begin when you're
50 to 75 yards out from the green.
This is the vale of tears.

Tony Lema

The chip is the greatest economist in golf.

Bobby Jones

The best golfers spend the most time
practicing — and they devote
the most time to their iron shots.

Lloyd Mangrum

Concentrate on hitting the green.
The cup will come to you.

Cary Middlecoff

No one has as much luck around the greens
as one who practices a lot.

Chi Chi Rodriguez

Golf is a game of precision, not strength.

Jack Nicklaus

It is nothing new or original to say that golf is played one stroke at a time. But it took me years to realize it.

Bobby Jones

Golf is not a game of great shots. It's a game of the most accurate misses.

Gene Littler

11

Putting

Putting is the stroke that separates the champions from the near greats. Efficiency around the greens is essential — when one's putter goes cold, so does one's golf game. For this reason, the putt is the most discussed shot in golf.

Champagne Tony Lema penned the following: "I rather suspect that more words have been written on the subject of putting, and more wild theories concocted than on any other phase of the game."

Putting is to golf what the end game is to chess. Lema called it "the ultimate stroke, the one that ends all discussion." The following gems of wisdom come courtesy of champions who have made more than their share of pressure putts. End of discussion.

You drive for show, and putt for dough.

Bobby Locke

The less said about the putter, the better.
Here is an element of torture.

Tony Lema

Putting allows the touchy golfer two to four
opportunities to blow a gasket in the short
space of two to forty feet.

Tommy Bolt

Putting affects the nerves more than anything.
I would actually get nauseated over
a three-footer.

Byron Nelson

You know those two-foot downhill putts with a break? I'd rather see a rattlesnake.

Sam Snead

Love and putting are mysteries for the philosopher to solve.
Both subjects are beyond golfers.

Tommy Armour

I'm having putting troubles.
But it's not the putter, it's the puttee.

Frank Beard

There is no tragedy in missing a putt, no matter how short.
All have erred in this respect.

Walter Hagen

You don't necessarily have to be a good golfer to be a good putter, but you have to be a good putter to be a good golfer.

Tony Lema

Among golfers the putter is usually known as the payoff club and how right that is! Putting is in fact a game in itself.

Bobby Locke

There is no similarity between golf and putting; they are two different games — one played in the air, and the other on the ground.

Ben Hogan

Putting is like wisdom — partly a natural gift and partly the accumulation of experience.

Arnold Palmer

The four-foot putt probably causes more
anxiety than any other stroke in golf.
You can't escape it.

Harvey Penick

I don't fear death, but I sure don't like those
three-footers for par.

Chi Chi Rodriguez

Yips don't seize the victim during a
practice round. It is a tournament disease.

Tommy Armour

The big trick in putting is not method — the
secret of putting is domination of the nerves.

Henry Cotton

The better you putt, the better you play.

Don January

Being free of doubt is just as necessary on
a short putt as any other shot.

Harvey Penick

Second guesses in putting are fatal.

Bobby Locke

Confidence is the key to putting.

Tony Lema

A putt cannot go in the hole if it's short.
I'd rather face a four-footer coming back than
leave the ball on the front lip.

Tom Watson

Ninety percent of putts
that are short don't go in.

Yogi Berra

M ost fine putters are putters
subconsciously. Putting is a psychology,
not a system.

Mickey Wright

T reat each putt as a separate little task
without worrying about what has gone
before or what will come after.

Bernhard Langer

T o sink the ball in the hole, you must think
the ball in the hole.

Bob Rosburg

M ake what you want of it, but it's all on the
greens — and half of that's in your head.

Tom Weiskopf

In standing over a putt,
my first priority is comfort.

Bob Charles

Solid contact is as important with your
putter as it is with your five-iron.

Nick Price

In golf, the first thing that leaves you
is your putting.

Gene Sarazen

A sure way to break a bad putting spell
is to get on the practice green and
return to the fundamentals.

Bob Rosburg

You can tell a good putt
by the noise it makes.

Bobby Locke

12

Winning & Losing

The legendary football coach Knute Rockne proclaimed, "The price for victory is hard work." Rockne's words may hold true on the football field, but winning golf requires more. Cool nerves and savvy course management are also necessities.

Gene Sarazen, fresh from a win over Walter Hagen, was hospitalized for an emergency appendectomy. Commenting on his victory from the hospital bed, Sarazen confessed, "A sick appendix is not as difficult to deal with as a five-foot putt." Five-foot putts often represent the thin line between victory and defeat. For the squeamish player, those five feet can seem like five miles.

If you'd like to know more about winning — or how to avoid the alternative — read on. You'll learn that the price of victory *is* hard work, with a few other things thrown in for good measure.

Winners are different.
>> They're a different breed of cat.

>>> *Byron Nelson*

The biggest thing is to have the mind-set and
the belief that you can win every tournament.
Nicklaus had it.

>>> *Tiger Woods*

The human element in the shape of an
opponent is essential. Always play for
something, no matter how small,
even though it only be a black cigar.

>>> *Walter J. Travis*

I love competition so much that
when I'm alone, I compete with myself.

>>> *Bruce Lietzke*

Handling pressure is the difference
    between winning and losing.

Raymond Floyd

My formula for success is simple:
    practice and concentration — then more
    practice and more concentration.

Babe Didrikson Zaharias

There is a philosophy of boldness — to take
    advantage of every tiny opening
    toward victory.

Arnold Palmer

Every tournament has its climax,
    its winning moment. If you're not watchful,
    you will miss it and lose your best chance.

Peter Thomson

Over the first three rounds you're playing
the course. In the final round, if you're in
contention, you're playing the man.

Jack Nicklaus

Great champions have an enormous sense
of pride. The people who excel are those who
are driven to show the world—and prove to
themselves — just how good they are.

Nancy Lopez

In a major championship, you don't care
about the money. You're just trying to get
your name on a piece of silver — that's all
you're trying to do.

Nick Faldo

No one remembers who came in second.

Walter Hagen

You hear that winning breeds winning.
But no — winners are bred from losing.
They learn that they don't like it.

Tom Watson

There are two kinds of golf: golf and
tournament golf. They are not the same.

Bobby Jones

I only bet a quarter, but I play each shot
as if it were for a championship.

Walter J. Travis

A good golfer has the determination to win
and the patience to wait for the breaks.

Gary Player

I play to win. I don't see any reason to play
any other way.

Tiger Woods

In golf, you have to learn to win by yourself.
That's why golf is the greatest game. You win
by yourself and you win *for* yourself.

Tom Watson

Golf is a game of misses and the winners
are those who have the best misses.

Kathy Whitworth

Golf is a game measured in yards, but the
difference between a hit and a miss is
calipered in micro-millimeters.

Tony Lema

No one becomes a champion without help.

Johnny Miller

Take less time to read the scorecard and
more time to read the hole.

Chi Chi Rodriguez

The PGA tour isn't pressure.
Pressure is playing for $10 when you
don't have a dime in your pocket.

Lee Trevino

If I had to cram all my
tournament experience
into one sentence,
I would say,
"Don't give up and
don't let up!"

Tony Lema

13

Life

Life is Like a Round of Golf

Life is like a round of golf
With many a turn and twist.
But the game is much too sweet and short
To curse the shots you've missed.

Sometimes you'll hit it straight and far,
Sometimes the putts roll true.
But each round has its errant shots
And troubles to play through.

So always swing with courage
No matter what the lie.
And never let the hazards
Destroy the joy inside.

And keep a song within your heart.
Give thanks that you can play.
For the round is much too short and sweet
To let it slip away.

by Criswell Freeman

When it comes to the game of life,
  I figure I've played the whole course.

Lee Trevino

The most rewarding things you do in life
  are often the ones that look
    like they can't be done.

Arnold Palmer

Golf is a lot like life.
  When you make a decision, stick with it.

Byron Nelson

It's not how fast you get there,
  but how long you stay.

Patty Berg

You are what you think
you are, in golf and in life.

Raymond Floyd

They say golf is like life
but don't believe them.
Golf is more complicated
than that.

Gardner Dickinson

That's life.
The older you get, the tougher it is to score.

Bob Hope

It's better to be 70 years young
than 40 years old.

Gary Player

Life consists of a lot of minor annoyances
and a few matters of real consequence.

Harvey Penick

Even if you aren't having an extra good day,
always count your blessings.
Be thankful you are able to be out on a
beautiful course. Most people in the world
don't have that opportunity.

Fred Couples

In golf, as in life, you get out of it
what you put into it.

Sam Snead

Being able to help people and give back —
that's what life is all about.

Tiger Woods

Match your strategy to your skills.

Arnold Palmer

There are no blind holes
the second time you play them.

Tommy Armour

Alas! The world is still
a testy par five.

Jim Murray

Don't hurry. Don't worry.
You're only here for a
short visit. So don't forget
to stop and smell
the roses.

Walter Hagen

<u>14</u>

Observations
on Golf, Fresh Air,
Pleasant Partners
& Other Necessities of Life

We conclude with a potpourri of wisdom
from and about the links. Enjoy.

Golf, like measles, should be caught young.
P. G. Wodehouse

Golf reflects the cycle of life.
No matter what you shoot, the next day you
have to go back to the first tee and begin all
over again and make yourself into something.
Peter Jacobsen

Give me golf clubs, fresh air and
a beautiful partner, and you can keep
the clubs and the fresh air.
Jack Benny

Golf is the only sport where the ball
doesn't move until you hit it.
Ted Williams

How has retirement affected my golf game?
A lot more people beat me now.
Dwight D. Eisenhower

I don't have a handicap. I'm *all* handicap.
Lyndon Baines Johnson

I'll know I'm getting better at golf because
I'm hitting fewer spectators.
Gerald Ford

Whenever I play with Gerald Ford, I try to
make it a foursome — the president, myself,
a paramedic and a faith healer.
Bob Hope

Because of the suit I was wearing,
  I couldn't make a good pivot on the swing.
  And I had to hit the ball with one hand.

Alan Shepard
describing his famous golf shot on the moon

Every hole should be a difficult par
  and a comfortable bogey.

Robert Trent Jones, Sr.

A parent never dies.
  He or she lives in your heart.

Robert Trent Jones, Jr.

A light, tender, sensitive touch
  is worth a ton of brawn.

Peter Thomson

Some of us worship in churches,
some in synagogues, some on golf courses.

Adlai Stevenson

The only time my prayers are never answered
is on the golf course.

Billy Graham

It is not mere technical skill that makes
a man a golfer, it is the golfing soul.

P. G. Wodehouse

No one ever conquers golf.

Kathy Whitworth

You never master golf.
You take what it gives, and you learn from it.

Charlie Sifford

There is more to life than golf. I've always
had to finish my homework before playing.

Tiger Woods

That little white ball is always staring back
at you, daring you to make a mistake.

Sam Snead

There are two things that won't last long in
this world, and that's dogs chasing cars
and pros putting for pars.

Lee Trevino

Nothing goes down slower
  than a golf handicap.

Bobby Nichols

The average golfer doesn't play golf.
  He attacks it.

Jack Burke, Jr.

If it weren't for golf,
  I'd probably be a caddie today.

George Archer

Golfers find it a very trying matter
  to turn at the waist, more particularly
  if they have a lot of waist to turn.

Harry Vardon

If there is a fountain of youth,
it has to be exercise.

Gary Player

The secret to longevity is keeping your
weight down, not smoking, limiting your
toddies and getting plenty of rest.

Tommy Bolt

Retire to what? I'm a golfer and a fisherman.
I've got no place to retire to.

Julius Boros

I never wanted to be a millionaire.
I just wanted to live like one.

Walter Hagen

All other things being equal,
greens break to the west.

Ben Hogan

Golfer's Wisdom

I learn something new about the game
almost every time I step on the course.

Ben Hogan

Luck? Sure. But only after long practice and
only with the ability to think under pressure.

Babe Didrikson Zaharias

Make the hard ones look easy
and the easy ones look hard.

Walter Hagen

Golfers have analyzed the game in order
to find "the secret." There is no secret.

Henry Cotton

The sweetest two words are "next time."
The sourest word is "if."

Chi Chi Rodriguez

I can sum it up like this:
Thank God for
the game of golf.

Arnold Palmer

Sources

Index of Sources
(All Sources Are Championship Golfers
Unless Otherwise Noted)

About the Author

Criswell Freeman is a Doctor of Clinical Psychology living in Nashville, Tennessee. He is the author of *When Life Throws You a Curveball, Hit It* and The Wisdom Series from WALNUT GROVE PRESS.

About Wisdom Books

Wisdom Books chronicle memorable quotations in an easy-to-read style. Written by Criswell Freeman, this series provides inspiring, thoughtful and humorous messages from entertainers, athletes, scientists, politicians, clerics, writers and renegades. Each title focuses on a particular region or area of special interest.

Combining his passion for quotations with extensive training in psychology, Dr. Freeman revisits timeless themes such as perseverance, courage, love, forgiveness and faith.

"Quotations help us remember the simple yet profound truths that give life perspective and meaning," notes Freeman. "When it comes to life's most important lessons, we can all use gentle reminders."

The Wisdom Series
by Dr. Criswell Freeman

Regional Titles

Sports Titles

Special Interest Titles

Wisdom Books are available through booksellers everywhere. For information about a retailer near you, call 1-800-256-8584.